I am a
Hindu

James Nixon

Photography by Chris Fairclough

W
FRANKLIN WATTS
LONDON·SYDNEY

First published in 2007 by
Franklin Watts
338 Euston Road
London NW1 3BH

Franklin Watts Australia
Level 17/207 Kent Street
Sydney NSW 2000

501196267

ISBN: 978 0 7496 7446 5 (hbk)
ISBN: 978 0 7496 7458 8 (pbk)

Dewey classification number: 294'.5

A CIP catalogue record for this book is available from the British Library.

Planning and production by Discovery Books Limited
Editor: James Nixon
Designer: Ian Winton
Photography: Chris Fairclough
Series advisors: Diana Bentley MA and Dee Reid MA,
Fellows of Oxford Brookes University

The author, packager and publisher would like to thank the following
people for their participation in this book: Bhranti and Kirtie Parekh and family;
Gujarat Hindu Society, Preston.

All photographs by Chris Fairclough.

Printed in China

Franklin Watts is a division of Hachette Children's books,
an Hachette Livre UK company.

Contents

I am a Hindu

My name is Bhranti and I am a Hindu.

Hindus believe in
one God who has
many forms.

orms of our God

We pray to Vishnu for protection.

Vishnu

6

We pray to
Hanuman the
monkey god for
good luck.

Going to worship

My family worship God at the mandir.

I take flowers with
me, to give to God.

At the mandir

Before we enter we take off our shoes...

...and ring
the bell.

Praising God

We show our love for God in many ways.

We chant prayers,
and we sing and
clap our hands.

The shrine

We have a shrine at home.

I pray in front of it
and think about God.

God's teachings

God tells us to live a good life.

16

We must help others
and work hard.

Vegetarian food

My family only eat vegetarian food.

I like the
chickpeas best.

Festivals

Hindus have many festivals. At Holi we light a bonfire.

At Diwali we light
candles to praise God.

God loves me

I am happy to
be a Hindu.

I know God loves me.

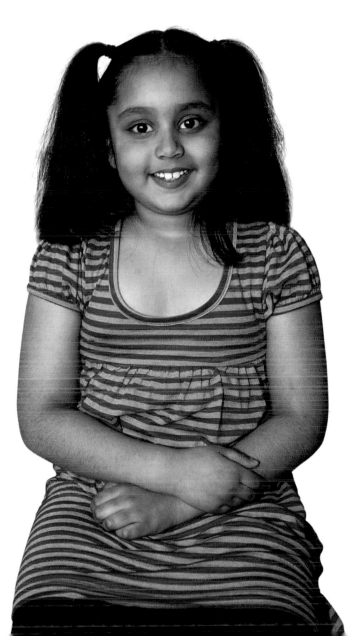

Word bank

Look back for these words and pictures.

Bonfire

Candles

Chant

Chickpeas

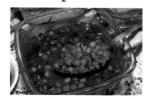

Diwali

Hanuman

Holi

Mandir

Pray

Shrine

Vegetarian

Vishnu